Anonymous

The Saint Louis Union Station

A monograph

Anonymous

The Saint Louis Union Station
A monograph

ISBN/EAN: 9783744646680

Printed in Europe, USA, Canada, Australia, Japan

Cover: Foto ©Andreas Hilbeck / pixelio.de

More available books at **www.hansebooks.com**

THE

St. Louis Union Station

A Monograph

BY THE

ARCHITECT AND OFFICERS

OF THE

Terminal Railroad Association

OF ST. LOUIS

※

MDCCCLXXXXV

NATIONAL CHEMIGRAPH COMPANY,
I. HAAS & CO., Selling Agents,
ST. LOUIS, MO.

No. 313

of a numbered edition of

one thousand copies.

PRESENTED TO

_____

_____

WITH THE COMPLIMENTS OF

_____

THE GRAND
STAIRCASE
PENN STATION

THE
TERMINAL RAILROAD
ASSOCIATION
OF
ST. LOUIS.

Tower Group from West Balcony.

EXECUTIVE OFFICERS, BOARD OF DIRECTORS
AND EXECUTIVE COMMITTEE.

WILLIAM TAUSSIG, President. JULIUS S. WALSH, Vice-President.

DIRECTORS.

M. E. INGALLS. C. M. HAYS. W. B. DODDRIDGE. W. W. PEABODY.

E. P. BRYAN. C. G. WARNER.

EXECUTIVE COMMITTEES.

1890, 1891 and 1892.

J. F. BARNARD, Chairman. C. M. HAYS. A. W. DICKINSON.

1893.

C. M. HAYS, Chairman. F. W. TRACY. GEO. C. SMITH.

1894.

C. M. HAYS, Chairman. W. B. DODDRIDGE. E. P. BRYAN.

FINANCIAL AGENTS.

J. P. MORGAN & COMPANY, New York.

7

TERMINAL RAILROAD ASSOCIATION OF ST. LOUIS.

GENERAL AND OPERATIVE OFFICERS.

GENERAL OFFICERS.

Jos. Ramsey, Jr., General Manager.   Jas. Hanna, Auditor and Secretary.

M. F. Watts, Counsel.   F. C. Daab, Cashier.   J. E. Williams, Purchasing Agt.

TRANSPORTATION DEPARTMENT.

W. A. Garrett, Superintendent.   E. A. Chenery, Sup't Telegraph.

H. M. Smith, Master Mechanic.

J. J. Coakley, Station Master.

H. Lihou, Union Station Ticket Agt.   Wm. Steele, Union Station Baggage Agt.

CONSTRUCTION AND MAINTENANCE DEPARTMENT.

H. P. Taussig, Chief Engineer.

J. W. Taylor, Ass't Engineer in charge Construction.

N. W. Rayrs, Superintendent Bridges and Structures.

G. B. Ross, Electrician.   John Wynn Road Master.

TRAFFIC DEPARTMENT.

V. W. Fisher, Passenger and Ticket Agent.

S. D. Webster, Claim Agent.   J. L. Penney, Commercial Agent.

F. X. Roederer, Freight Agent.

8

PLAT OF
ST. LOUIS AND EAST ST. LOUIS.
SHOWING
RAILWAY SYSTEM
OF THE
TERMINAL R. R. ASSOC. OF ST. LOUIS.
Scale

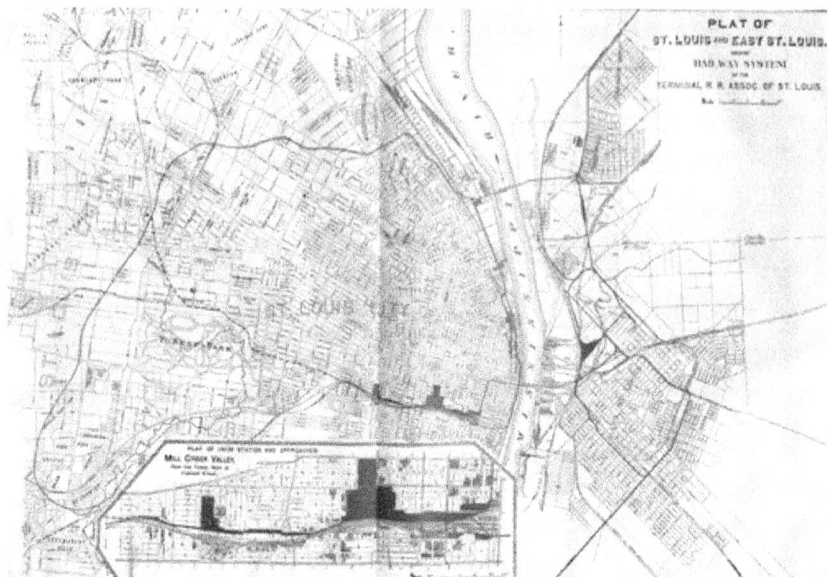

PLAT OF
ST. LOUIS AND EAST ST. LOUIS.
HALF-WAY SYSTEM
TERMINAL R. R. ASSOC. OF ST. LOUIS.

BAGGAGE HOUSE.

POWER HOUSE.

Theo. C. Link, Architect.

Panoramic View of Town from Reservoir

WEST END OF GRAND HALL.

THEO. C. LINK, Architect.

9

ABLE OF CONTENTS

Suspended Ceiling of Grand Hall.

IST OF CHEMIGRAPH PLATES.

ILLUSTRATIONS IN THE TEXT.

Electrolier on Market Street.

PART I.

PART II.

PART III.

PART IV.

ILLUSTRATIONS IN THE TEXT—CONTINUED.

Painting of the Eads Bridge in Private Dining-Room.

INTRODUCTION.

TERMINAL RAILROAD ASSOCIATION OF ST. LOUIS,

OFFICE OF THE PRESIDENT,

St. Louis, January 1st, 1895.

THIS memorial presentation of a great work has been prepared, mainly, for the use and information of our railroad friends and the professional public, but also in justice to the officers of this Company and others, whose labors, talents and enthusiasm have contributed so much to its successful completion.

In reviewing the history of the enterprise—from its inception to its final reality—it is proper to state that there is in the country no city of the size of St. Louis which has all its railway lines pouring out their entire passenger traffic at one common point. There are twenty-two different lines of railroads—thirteen from the East and nine from the West—which converge here. The greater portion of their traffic is interchanging. Every train from the East brings passengers for the West, and *vice versa*. The vast number of daily passengers to whom this Station is a resting-place in

14

a transcontinental journey gives a variety and a color to the assembling crowds and imposes conditions for their accommodation and comfort such as do not exist elsewhere.

Casual observers have only a faint idea of the large aggregation of human life which unfolds itself daily at this Station. The traffic is cosmopolitan in every sense. Passengers from every portion of the globe, speaking every language and destined for every section of the country, come and go here. Their needs, from the most fastidious to the most lowly, must have attention, and to cover all the necessities of the case and fulfill all its conditions the arrangements made had to be planned on the most liberal and comprehensive scale.

The professional and mechanical devices which were adopted for the operation of trains, and for the promptness and absolute safety of their movements, are the results of the most modern and advanced thought in that direction, and when it is considered, as is more specifically related further on, in the chapter on interlocking, that 247 distinct movements of trains and engines, or over four per minute, are made in one hour while handling the heavy traffic concentrated in the morning and evening of each day, the exacting nature of the service, and the skill required for it, may be measured.

The site was determined upon by the Board of Directors on April 1st, 1890, after the merits of many other locations had been carefully considered. In view of the fact that there are no through trains from any line running beyond St. Louis; that each line, from East or West, made the end of its run at the Station and there transferred its passengers destined beyond St. Louis to other lines; and in view of the peculiar topographical conditions of our city, which confined its railway approaches within a comparatively narrow valley and made the operation of such a vast number of passenger trains within that valley extremely difficult and dangerous, it was concluded by a majority of the Board (some of its members dissenting) to adopt the "End Station" plan, instead of the continuous "Through Station" plan, on which the old depot was constructed.

On the site selected there were situated many large industrial establishments and over one hundred houses, many of them four-story substantial brick buildings. Among the former were one of the largest breweries in the city, occupying with its imposing build-

THE GRAND HALL.
Opening Night—Flash-light Photo by Alester.

THEO. C. LINK, Architect.

16

ings almost a square of ground; a large flour mill; the complete plant, with gasometer, of one of our gas companies; one of the largest soap and candle factories; a wagon factory; stores, warehouses, and the car stables and sheds of an extensive city car line.

The franchise from the city was obtained in February, 1892, and in April following the demolition of the buildings and excavation were commenced. On account of the nature of the ground which formed part of the old Chouteau pond or lake, great difficulties had to be overcome in building the heavy foundation walls; the old vaults under the brewery had to be blown with dynamite to make room for the walls and piers, and most of the piers on which the steel columns of the shed rest had to have pile foundations. It took more than a year to complete the foundation walls, and not until July 8th, 1893, was the corner-stone laid of the building proper.

On September 1st, 1894, fourteen months after the laying of the corner-stone, the building was completed in all its details, ready for public use, and on that day it was dedicated and opened with appropriate ceremonies. The train service commenced that same night— the first train entering the Station at 1:45 a. m. on September 2d, and the service has been uninterruptedly carried on since with the utmost regularity.

The building, the Arcade or Midway between it and the train shed, and the train shed itself, occupy an area of 497,092 square feet, or 11.1 acres. The ground south of the train shed, between it and the power-house, on which all the express, baggage and mail cars are handled, and which commands the approaches from the main tracks, contains 465,970 square feet, making a total area for the station itself, exclusive of all main track approaches, of 963,062 square feet, or 20 acres. The area covered by the four main tracks, reaching from

The West Approach.

the tunnel to Grand Avenue, including the proposed storage yard on Compton Avenue, all of which is exclusively set aside for passenger service, is 867,098 square feet, making a total of 1,830,360 square feet, or 42 acres, which goes into this new system, and nearly all of which has been purchased or acquired within the last three years. There are nineteen miles of track in this system, of which the 31 tracks under the train shed compose three and a half miles. In the power-house is contained all the machinery which provides the electric lighting, the interlocking switch and signal system, and for the steam heating of the entire establishment. The interlocking system is worked by 122 levers, controls 130 switches and 103 signals, and is the largest in the country. The electric light plant has a capacity of lighting 300 arc lights and 5,000 incandescent lights. The heating apparatus has a capacity to supply 44,500 square feet of radiating surface, amply sufficient for the Station proper, the express and baggage buildings and all the other buildings appurtenant to the Station. And, finally, the outlay required for the real estate and the improvements, as thus shortly described, is in the neighborhood of six and a half million dollars.

Distinct chapters describing the details of the various architectural, engineering and operating features of the entire system will be found in this volume, and supply much information of interest to the profession and the public.

A copy of the specifications for the building proper, as they were submitted to competing architects at home and abroad, is hereto attached, and also a copy of the official record showing the proceedings of the Board of Directors under which the award, from among eight competing designs, was given to Mr. Theo. C. Link, the architect, whose skill and genius have imprinted themselves on the monumental structure and its graceful and practical interior.

On the first page appear the names of the Directors of the company, of the members of its Executive Committee, and of the principal officers, whose labors were so freely given to this work. It would be presumptuous to praise them each in the measure of their merits, where each and all worked with a zeal and enthusiasm which are beyond all praise.

WM. TAUSSIG, President.

Original Perspective Submitted in the Competition by Theo. C. Link, Architect.

THE COMPETITION.

In March, 1891, ten architects in various parts of the United States were invited to submit drawings in accordance with the following instructions:

SITE. — The main building is to be for a stub-end station, situated fronting on Market Street, beginning at the southwest corner of Eighteenth Street, and extending along Market Street a distance of four hundred and fifty-five feet nine inches (455 ft, 9 in.). The depth of the building proper not to be greater than eighty feet (80 ft.). The ground covered, including building and sheds, will extend from the rear end of the main building between Eighteenth Street and Twentieth Street, covering the system of tracks as designated on accompanying blue print. All measurements as given on blue print governing spacing of tracks, platforms, the ends of tracks, distance from building, etc., shall govern the Architect in formulating his plans. The Market Street front is intended for general entrance, and the Eighteenth Street front for general exit. Partial exit to Twentieth Street, and facilities for reaching Baggage Rooms, should be provided for.

2. Competition will be open to Architects selected by the Board or its Executive Committee, and those submitting designs and specifications will be paid as below.

3. The plans and accompanying specifications are to be distinguished by a motto or device different from any previously used by the respective competitors, and when alternative designs are sent in, a different motto or device must be used for each. The plans and specifications are to be delivered to the address of Wm. Taussig, President, Union Depot, St. Louis, on or before July 1st, 1891, with a sealed envelope bearing outside the motto or device of the Architect submitting same and enclosing his name and address, which envelope will not be opened until after the Board of Directors of the Union Depot Company has finally selected one of the designs.

The following accommodations are to receive careful attention from the Architects in executing their plans —

MAIN FLOOR.

*General Hall or Waiting Room, 10,000 square feet.
Gentlemen's Waiting Room, 3,000 square feet.
Ladies' Waiting Room, 6,000 square feet.
Dining Hall, 3,000 square feet.
Ladies' Toilet and Package Rooms, Gentlemen's Smoking Room, News Stands, Telegraph
    Stand, Stairways, Elevators, etc.
*General Hall or Waiting Room is to have full clear-story.

BASEMENT FLOOR SPACE.

Concourse, about 12,000 square feet.
Telegraph Office (R. R.), 2,000 square feet.
Restaurant, about 3,200 square feet.
Ticket Office, about 2,000 square feet.
Pullman Sleeping Car Ticket Office, 200 square feet.
Wagner Sleeping Car Ticket Office, 200 square feet.
Mail and Money Order Room, 500 square feet.
Emigrant Room, 7,000 square feet.
Remainder of space by Closets, Wash Room, Barber Shop, Baggage **Checking Room**, Depot Master's Office, Elevators, etc.

No plans will be considered which do not conform to the following rules:

1. All drawings to be **executed in India** ink only; no tinting allowed.
2. Horizontal and **vertical sections** of walls to be filled in black, and must be free from cross-etching.
3. **Plans**, except as hereinafter specified in brackets, to be drawn to a uniform scale of one-eighth of an inch **to the foot**.
4. Each set of plans to be accompanied by a complete specification and estimate of cost.
5. Special reference must be had to the following requirements:
   A. The general lay-out of tracks and platforms to facilitate the handling of mail, express and baggage **matter** from and to trains, and the egress and ingress of passengers.
   B. Convenience in arrangement of the main and basement floors, as regards the public and official uses thereof.
   C. Lighting, heat, ventilation and drainage.
6. **Architects must submit** drawings as follows, on Whatman's paper, linen mounted:
   One block plan of site, showing all tracks, sheds and building, on a scale of fifty feet to one inch.
   Plan of each floor, on a scale of one-eighth of an inch to the foot.
   One longitudinal section.
   One transverse section.
   One front elevation.
   One side elevation.
   One rear elevation.
   One prospective view (line drawing), showing the two main fronts, and drawn on a plane at the corner of Eighteenth and Market Streets. A deviation from this will be considered sufficient cause for a rejection of the design. Line shading allowed. The drawing must be made on a scale of one-eighth inch to the foot, or one-sixteenth inch to the foot and then enlarged to one-eighth by photography.
7. A specification for each of the following departments of work must be furnished: Excavation, masonry, brick **work**, iron work, carpenter work, hardware, plastering, roofing, plumbing, drainage, gas-fitting, galvanized iron, copper and **tin**, painting and glazing, heating and ventilation, gas and electric fixtures, and fresco decorations.
8. Architects must examine the site in person.
9. The building to be constructed of such material as may be selected by invited Architects. The main floor to be fire-proof throughout. Basement and first floor to be fire-proof. Everything above main floor to be constructed on the slow combustion plan.
10. Arrangements are to be made for all the other necessary water-closets, lavatories, vaults, elevators, and all other desirable appointments and fittings of the latest style, so as to render the building complete in every particular for the purpose for which it is intended, s. e., a Union Station of the First Class.
11. All floors above the main floor to be arranged for office purposes.
12. Plans for the shed and auxiliary buildings, designed so as to bring about the best results and to give uniformity to the architectural features of the whole, must accompany the plans for the main building, but need not be carried out in detail.
13. Compensation will be as follows:
    A. The Architect to whose design shall be awarded the first premium and whose plans are accepted shall receive a commission not exceeding ten thousand dollars ($10,000), and for this sum he shall furnish the Board of Directors all general drawings, specifications and complete details which they may deem necessary to carry out the construction of the main building and the general designs for sheds and auxiliary buildings. He shall also furnish the Superintendent all the information and advice he may require at all times during the progress of the work, and for all time that he may have to be personally at the building he shall receive the sum of ten dollars ($10) per day for his services and expenses; Provided, that such personal attention shall not be owing to any defect in the plans and specifications given at the request of the Superintendent in charge of the building.
    B. **The** Architect to whom shall be awarded the second premium to receive fifteen hundred dollars ($1,500), and **the** Architect to whom shall be awarded the third premium to receive one thousand dollars ($1,000); Provided, that these plans shall remain the property of the company.
    C. **The** other competing Architects to receive five hundred dollars ($500) each.
    D. Where changes are made in the original plans **as** accepted, prior to detail plans being furnished, no charge will be allowed to the Architect for the extra **work** in getting out the revised details.
14. A competent Superintendent will be appointed by the Board of Directors to supervise the construction of the work.

THE PRIVATE DINING ROOM.

Looking West.

THEO. C. LINK, Architect.

21

On July 1st, 1891, eight sets of drawings were received, and the Board of Directors proceeded to examine them.

Following is a transcript from the proceedings of the Board of Directors at its meeting held July, 1891:

All the members being present, Mr. Barnard in the Chair, eight plans, bearing devices and mottoes as undernoted, were submitted for examination, to wit: "Lion Rampant," car wheel marked "Hermes," "Gare," "Palmam qui meruit ferat," "Etruscan Vase," "Dulce," "Gray brick and Redford stone," and "Liberty."

After a careful examination of the several plans, two ballots were taken to ascertain the general sense of the committee, and, as the result of such balloting, it was unanimously

RESOLVED, That the premiums for the three best plans, as provided in the "Instructions to Architects," be awarded as follows:

"ETRUSCAN VASE," First Premium. $10,000 00
"LIBERTY," Second Premium. 1,500 00
"GARE," Third Premium. 1,000 00

In presence of the Board, the Secretary then proceeded to open the sealed envelopes containing the names of the authors of the several plans, when it was found that the first premium had been awarded to THEODORE C. LINK, OF ST. LOUIS, the second to Grable & Weber, of St. Louis, and the third to Van Brunt & Howe, of Kansas City.

JAMES HANNA, Secretary.

Mr. Link was instructed to proceed at once with the work, and at a subsequent meeting of the Board of Directors he was appointed Superintendent of Construction, and given entire control of all work upon the Headhouse, including the decoration.

Original Drawing for Grand Hall.

Scagliola Column in General Waiting-
Room.

24

ST. LOUIS UNION STATION ON

MARKET STREET.

THEO. C. LINK, Architect.

PART I.

THE HEADHOUSE.

N reading the instructions to competing architects, it is quite evident that much thought and study had been bestowed upon the subject by the Board of Directors and officers of the Terminal Railroad Association before it was placed in the hands of the architects. A definite scheme had been outlined and the requirements clearly stated.

The architects' work consisted in the rational arrangement and disposition of parts, considered both from a utilitarian and artistic standpoint.

The original design contemplated a building 455 feet 9 inches long by 80 feet wide generally, and the first plans were drawn to cover this area only. During the progress of construction, the property immediately adjoining the building on the west was acquired, adding 150 feet to the structure and necessitating a revision of its western termination. This explains the discrepancy between the design originally adopted and that exhibited in the executed structure.

This subsequent acquisition of additional property, however, did not materially affect the floor plans, which remain unchanged in all essential points, the additional 150 feet by 80 feet being designed for the use of hotel and stores.

Window Detail of East Pavilion.

The total frontage of the Headhouse on Market Street is now 606 feet, extending from Eighteenth to Twentieth Street, by an average depth of 80 feet from north to south.

The general front line of the building is 40 feet south of the south line of Market Street, but this space is partly broken by the terraced approaches, the vestibules and a porte cochère.

The ground floor, the entire first story and the floors of second story are fire-proof.

A free treatment of the Romanesque style has been selected as the one pre-eminently adapted to express, by historical associations, the character and purpose of the structure.

In this day the railway station is as much the means of entrance and exit to a city as was the bastioned gate of mediæval times. It is therefore intended as a modern elaboration of the feudal gateway.

The Grand Central Hall, with the principal entrances, is strongly accentuated, while the two upper stories of offices are recessed with a strong determination to subdue the commercial and heighten the monumental effect of the composition.

The east pavilion, grouped together with the clock tower on the highest point of the site, forms the eastern termination of the building, the western termination being strongly marked by a gable projecting beyond the general building line some ten feet.

The tower is 230 feet high, measured from the track level, and has four clock dials, ten feet in diameter.

The principal façades on Market and Eighteenth Streets are faced with Bedford (Indiana) limestone, backed with red bricks. The south and west walls are of gray bricks above and of buff Roman bricks below the roof of the train shed. The roofs are

27

THE EAST APPROACH.   THEO. C. LINK, Architect.

28

covered with Spanish tiles of a color to match the stone walls, on the theory that a monochrome will aid in attaining the effect of loftiness.

Considerable difficulty was encountered in the construction of the foundations. On the eastern portion the ground was undermined for some distance with a network of caves and vaults, the interesting remains of the oldest brewery in the city. These subterraneous passages were below the sewer system, and filled with water immediately after being exposed. Toward the center of the building excellent ground was encountered, while the western end led us directly into an arm of the historic Chouteau Pond, where willow stumps, log cabins and the hulls of primitive boats were encountered twenty feet below the surface. This region was formerly famous for its springs, and an inconvenient number of them caused much vexatious delay by their sudden appearance.

The footings are of concrete throughout, the only exceptions being a few instances in which steel cantilevers were resorted to, the conditions being, however, quite exceptional. Not a pile was driven under the Head-house, though the temptation to use them at the western end was very great.

The Clock Tower.

The tower foundation is entirely disconnected from the balance of the foundations—in fact, the entire tower stands isolated, slip-joints being introduced between it and all abutting walls. Allowance was made for a settlement of one-half inch, but to date it has settled only one-quarter inch more than adjoining walls.

The foundation walls are carried up with Grafton rock, terminating with a granite base at the grade line.

The point of paramount importance in a railway station is its plan. Everything else is subservient to it. The directness, simplicity and straightforwardness of our station is its chief merit.

29

Arcade under East Arch, Grand Hall.

The difference in grades between the track level and the surrounding streets presented itself as a problem, rather difficult of solution, for the adjustment of easy and convenient ingress and egress.

Market Street has a fall of fifteen feet from Eighteenth Street to Twentieth Street. The track level is fifteen feet below the corner of Eighteenth and Market Streets, but on the same level with Twentieth Street. Eighteenth Street falls from north to south about four feet in the depth of the building.

It was finally decided to locate the floor line of the ground floor on a level with the tracks, except in the carriage concourse, which was adjusted to the level of Market Street at the intersection of Nineteenth Street. The floor line of the first story is, therefore, elevated about five feet above the level of Market Street where it intersects with Eighteenth Street. These conditions compelled a lower story height for the ground floor than would otherwise have been adopted, viz.: eighteen feet.

Detail of Arcaded Gallery, Grand Hall.

The two main floors, the ground floor and first story (aggregating about 70,000 square feet) are entirely devoted to the accommodation and comfort of the traveling public, and the arrangement of the rooms is the result of much study, and a full appreciation of their specific uses.

The central feature of each story is a great hall, 76 feet by 120 feet, from which one enters the minor apartments to the right and left. The central hall of the lower story, or the ground floor, called the "General Waiting-Room," has along its four walls the windows for the sale of railroad and sleeping

THE GRAND HALL.
Looking East.

THEO. C. LINK, Architect.

31

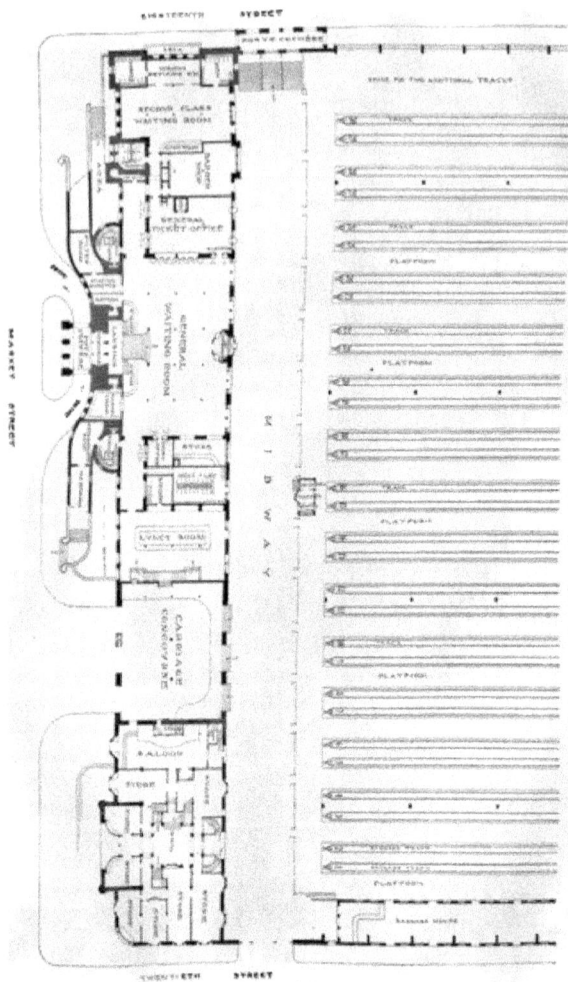

PLAN OF GROUND FLOOR
SAINT LOVIS VNION STATION
THEO C·LINK·ARCHITECT

car tickets, the telegraph and public telephone offices, a bureau of information, a substation of the United States Post Office, a parcel check-room, news, cigar, fruit and candy stands. The east corridor leads to the barber-shop, the bath-rooms, and to a waiting-room for second-class travelers. The west corridor leads to the lunch counters and a toilet-room for men. West of the lunch-room is the carriage concourse separating the station from the hotel annex.

On the two north corners of these central halls are round towers, which contain the elevators and staircases for the office floors, provision being made for carrying invalids in rolling-chairs from the basement to the first story in these elevators.

The two central halls are connected by the grand staircase. The platform of this staircase, which is half way between the two floors, is on a level with Market Street at that point, so that exits are provided from it. An arch of forty feet span over the grand staircase is made a decorative feature of special interest; it forms the framework to an allegorical picture in glass mosaic.

Another staircase connects the lunch-room on the ground floor with the general dining-room directly over it.

The entire first story is subdivided into waiting-rooms for such travelers as have to spend more or less time waiting for connections. Here everything has been done to enable them to pass the time pleasantly, and instructively for those who have an eye for form and color.

The central hall of the first story, called the "Grand Hall," is of magnificent proportions. Its barrel vaulted ceiling rises to a height of sixty-five feet above the floor.

The entire floor space to the east of the Grand Hall is set aside for the use of ladies. The first room from the Grand Hall is for ladies with gentlemen; adjoining this is a room for ladies exclusively, and part of this is again screened off as a retiring-room, furnished with lounges for emergency cases or invalids. The toilet and bath rooms

33

FIRST FLOOR PLAN·SAINT LOVIS VNION STATION·THEO·C·LINK·ARCHITECT·

electric fans located in a vault under the eastern part of the building, where it is again drawn over steam coils and forced into the rooms near the ceiling line under a pressure in excess of the atmospheric pressure on the outside. Auxiliary exhaust fans draw the foul air out of the rooms near the floor line, so that a constant change of air is maintained.

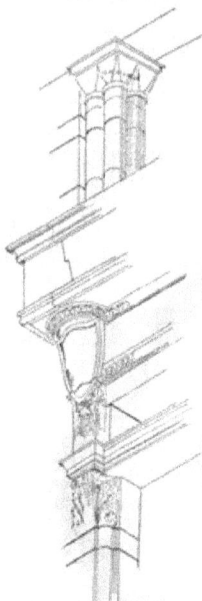

Electricity is used exclusively for power and illuminating purposes. With the exception of the Grand Hall, the private dining-room and in rooms where incandescent lamps are made to subserve decorative purposes, all waiting-rooms have arc lamps. There are about 3,500 incandescent and 150 arc lamps in the Headhouse, independent of the lamps in the Midway, the Train-shed, and Baggage-house. The Grand Hall has a wrought iron electrolier of twenty-foot spread, with 350 lamps. It is believed to be the largest chandelier in this country. The toilet arrangements are on an unusually liberal scale, the plumbing and marble work being of a quality equal to that usually encountered in a high-class hotel.

The settees and chairs in the waiting-rooms are especially designed in harmony with the character and decoration of the room.

The waiting-rooms and the principal offices have each one or more self-winding clocks, connected with and electrically controlled by a master clock in the Bureau of Information. Drinking fountains are placed throughout the waiting-rooms and halls, with cool and filtered water.

The restaurant, dining-rooms and offices have electro-automatic heat regulation.

Pneumatic tubes communicate between the telegraph offices and operators' room, and between the various station officials. A private telephone, with an exchange in the operators' room, connects the offices and rooms.

Detail of Balconies, East Pavilion.

Mail chutes deliver the letters from the offices to the post-office.

Drinking Fountain, Grand Hall.

For night service a watchman's check, with twenty-five stations, has been introduced.

All parts of the world have contributed to the fitting up of this great building. The mosaic floor of the ladies' room is of Belgian manufacture. The interlocking floor tile in the Grand Hall

36

THE GRAND STAIRCASE.   THEO. C. LINK, Architect.

37

The Upper Gallery.

and dining-room comes from England. Germany furnished the plain floor tile used in the basement and the enameled tile wainscot in the ladies' room. We have Numidian marble from Africa, Sienna and white marbles from Italy. The beautiful green marble called Vert Campagne comes from France. Alps green marble, from Switzerland, is in the Gothic Corridor; the toilet-room for men is of Georgia marble, and the lunch-room counter and wainscot of Tennessee marble. Vermont marble is used for steps and wainscot in the café, and the jet-black marble in the dining-room is a New York State product.

In the interior decoration of the building, the aim has been to produce quiet and harmonious effects with the simplest means possible.

An attempt is made throughout to suggest the character of the rooms in the materials, colors and decorations selected.

All waiting-rooms have dados of either marble, enameled tiles, or American faience. Oak wainscoting was used in the dining-hall and the waiting-room for ladies

Fireplace in Ladies Waiting-Room.

faience blocks. Between this and the bracketed frieze (eighteen feet from the floor line) the plain wall surfaces are lined with scagliola in tints and veinings of green and yellow. The brackets of the frieze, the capitals of the clustered columns, and other ornaments in relief, are touched with gold

exclusively, so as to impart to these rooms a homelike air.

In the entire ground floor, which is used for the transaction of business only, no attempt at elaboration of any kind has been made.

The Grand Hall on the first floor, however, demanded treatment which would intensify its architectural importance, and it is therefore made the *piece de resistance* of the structure. The walls start with a dado of dark green

38

leaf. The ornamental ribs' of the vaulted ceilings are covered solid with gold. The ceiling panels are painted in a greenish-yellow, enriched with stencil work. The deeply recessed background of the end arches and arcaded galleries is in a dull blue, giving them apparently immense depth and distance. The end walls of the Grand Hall are pierced with an arch of forty feet span. The sweep over the arch between a rich quirk bead in solid gold and the ceiling angle is decorated with low relief tracery emerging from female figures with torches in their uplifted hands. These figures are placed at radiating lines, seven on each wall. This relief work was placed there for the purpose of confining dust deposits where they will aid the design by intensifying certain lines of the ornament.

The corridor leading from the Grand Hall to the Dining-hall is interesting for its ceiling, which has the gothic fan tracery of the Tudor period; it is handled in strong colors. The Dining-hall is treated in rich tapestry effects on plain walls and ceiling panels, between stained oak beams and high wainscoting.

Smoking Room.

In character the private dining-room has the distinguished air of classic refinement. The effect lies more in its rich relief ornamentation, touched up with gold, than in the colors, which are of subdued hues.

39

ENTRANCE TO DINING HALL FROM GOTHIC CORRIDOR.   THEO. C. LINK, Architect.

40

In the smoking-room and the rooms for ladies color schemes appropriate to their respective uses were applied. The first room, for ladies with gentlemen, has a wainscoting of enameled German tile, and is all in cream, light pink and delicate blue, the perspective point being a fireplace of Numidian marble and a plaster niche in which poses the life-size form of a young girl holding the clock-dial in her outstretched arms.

The flat ornamentations throughout are stencil work, in some cases of very intricate design,

Ladies' Waiting-Room.

requiring ten or more colors to produce the effect desired, with the exception of the waiting-room for ladies exclusively, where a delicate frieze of roses by Mr. Fleury is introduced.

Acknowledgments are here due to the following gentlemen for valuable services rendered in their respective callings, viz.:

Messrs. Healy & Millet, of Chicago, who executed the color decorations of principal waiting-rooms; Mr. Porter White, of St. Louis, who executed the relief work in plaster from models by Mr. Wm. Bailey, of this city.

Mr. Robert Bringhurst, sculptor, who modeled the figures; and Messrs. Davis & Chambers, of St. Louis, who executed all the stained glass and Venetian mosaic work in the building.

The Hotel has about one hundred rooms, and is designed to be managed on the European plan. The first story corridor communicates directly with the dining-rooms in the Station, and there is no kitchen maintained in it. On the ground floor there are eight stores that can be entered from the streets, from the Midway and from the passage which leads from Market Street to the track platforms, and which is to be kept open to the public day and night.

Its construction is such that it can at any subsequent time be converted and arranged for depot purposes.

In its entirety the new Union Station is a small city in itself.

PART II.

THE TRAIN SHED.

The Train Shed is not only the largest existing, but it also covers the greatest number of tracks and serves the trains of more railway companies than any other train shed, as the following comparative table shows :

STATION.	LENGTH	BREADTH	AREA SQUARE FT.	TRACKS	COMPANIES
Union Station, St. Louis,	700	606	424,200	31	22
Boston & Maine, Boston,	596	460	246,560	23	3
St. Pancras, London,	700	240	168,000		
Frankfort, Germany,	600	552	331,200	18	4
Broad Street, Philadelphia,	592	304	179,986	16	1
Union Station, Chicago,	1,100	105	115,500	9	4
Philadelphia & Reading, Philadelphia,	800	260	208,000	14	
Dearborn Street, Chicago,	590	169	99,710	10	6
Grand Central, New York,	600	332	205,820	11	3
Cologne, Germany,	765	276	211,000	10	4

In the construction of a train shed covering so vast an area, it was very important to reduce the number of supports as well as the height of the structure to a minimum, so that in its completeness it would not overshadow the Headhouse, immediately north of it. We were therefore limited in its height, so that the apex of the skylight in the center of the roof should not exceed 100 feet. In general appearance, the structure finally adopted, from the exterior, gives the effect of one sweeping

"Train Shed.

Theo. C. Link, Architect.

The Baggage Run.

arch supported on columns. The top of the roof at the side is twenty-nine feet from track level; these points connected by a circular arch with a radius of 866 feet, will best convey the general appearance of this structure. The ends of the train shed are faced with corrugated iron, draped to cover the trusses; with an apron extending to within twenty feet of the track level, in which is set corrugated glass in sheets varying in length from forty feet to nothing. Over this roof are projecting ventilating and lighting bay segments in alternate panels of thirty feet width, stretching across the entire roof, with the exception of ninety feet on each side; these project ten feet above the general roof, the sides filled in with corrugated glass, three-eighths inch thick, set in T's with corrugated iron caps; the entire roof is covered with dressed two-inch flooring, with the dressed side exposed under the shed. Upon this decking the entire roof was again covered with American tin, manufactured in St. Louis. All that portion of the roof below the projecting bays was laid with standing seams to provide for expansion and contraction. The spaces between the bays and the roofs of the bays are all covered with flat seamed work. On the sides ample gutters are provided in the roof. The drainage of this vast area—almost ten acres—was provided for by means of down spouts every thirty feet on each side of the structure.

The Avenue of Bumpers.

In the center of the shed throughout its entire length, additional light is provided by a skylight thirty-six feet wide, covered with corrugated glass three-eighths inch thick, supported by copper bars. The sides of the central skylight provide ample ventilation for the structure.

Looking at the interior of this shed, it will be found that the space covered is divided into five spans; the two outer, each 90 feet 8 inches between centers of columns; the two immediately adjoining these, each 139 feet 2¾ inches; and the center span 141 feet 3½ inches. The two outer spans, of 90 feet 8 inches, have straight top chords and draped bottom chords; the two immediately adjoining and the center span, owing to the curvature of the roof, are of one length, the top chord conforming to the curve with a radius as mentioned

46

THE DINING HALL.

THEO. C. LINK, Architect.

47

before, and the bottom chord draped, so that all lower chord panels are of uniform length, all top chords of uniform length and all posts of one length throughout the entire structure for these three spans. The two side spans also have all top chords of one length and all bottom chords of one length.

The main train shed is 630 feet long, supported on columns at its outer lines every thirty feet. The intermediate lines of columns are spaced 60 feet apart lengthwise of the structure, supporting the intermediate trusses of the roof, by means of trusses connecting these columns. The shortest columns are 20 feet long; the longest 62 feet 3½ inches. The anchorage of the structure is entirely at the outer columns, which take care of all wind stresses. The intermediate columns are all pin connected at bottom. The only provision for expansion and contraction at the tops of the columns for the trusses is provided at each end of the center span depending on the anchorage of the outer

columns to their foundations against turning over. At the south end of this structure, the last span of 30 feet is thoroughly braced to the ground, forming towers, where columns exist, thus providing the necessary strength against wind strains in that direction.

In the designing of this structure, the stresses were calculated for dead load and snow to equal 40 pounds per square foot of vertical surface. The ground on which this structure was

Eighteenth Street Exit.

erected was formerly a part of the vast lake filled some twenty years ago with all manner of débris, making it necessary, on 64 of the 92 piers, to drive from 6 to 9 piles. These were driven with an 8,000-pound steam hammer to the proper depth, from 5 to 9 feet below the surface, before excavations were made. Concrete foundations were used throughout the entire work, made of Portland cement, all outer piers capped with Missouri granite, and the inner piers with Bedford limestone.

Construction work began on these foundations April 21st, 1892; the entire foundation was completed by September 23d of the same year. This required 10,855 lineal feet of piling, 3,013 cubic yards of excavation, and 1,477 yards of concrete; 44 granite caps and 48 Bedford limestone caps. The amount of steel used in the entire construction of the train shed was 5,471,721 pounds; of glass, 95,000 square feet; lumber, 961,000 feet board measure; and tin, 1,174 boxes. This includes the auxiliary shed, which lies north of the main train shed, having a uniform width of 70 feet for the entire width of the property, which, as was mentioned, is 606 feet, making a total area covered by the roof of 424,200 square feet.

The erection of the steel work was commenced July 7th, 1892, and the last truss was erected November 26th of the same year. All riveting was completed on March 31st, 1893, and the entire structure was ready for occupancy by November 25th of the same year.

THE MIDWAY.

The train shed proper begins seventy feet south of the south wall of the Headhouse, and covering the intervening space, known as the Midway, is a light steel trussed roof of glass and iron. This roof is above the second story of main waiting-room floor, so that from this floor a good view is obtained of every track, platform or train in the train shed.

From this vantage point at certain hours of the day as many as thirty trains may be seen at one time, ready to start on their journeys to all points of the compass, and all sections of the United States.

The Midway is well named; it is not only the midway space between the waiting-rooms and offices and the train platforms, or the midway point where friends "speed the parting and welcome the coming," but, like the great Midway of the "Dream City," coming through its numerous gates may be seen the peoples of all climes and nations.

It is fifty feet wide by 606 feet long and is separated from the train shed by a high ornamental wrought iron fence pierced by sixteen gates for ingress or egress to or from the train platforms. It is paved with granitoid. On the Eighteenth Street end of the Midway are a triple-arched exit and covered porte cochère. At the west end a large thirty-six foot arch leads to Twentieth Street. These exits are guarded by highly ornamented wrought iron gates.

Night Scene on the Midway.

Theo. C. Link, Architect.

PART III.

POWER HOUSE.

OUTH of the train shed is the Power House, containing the boilers, engines, dynamos, air compressors, and heating plant. It is located 1,687 feet from the Headhouse and on the central line of the train shed.

It is of brick, 67 feet by 134 feet, divided as follows: Beginning at the west end, boiler-room, 54 feet by 62 feet; steam heating apparatus, 20 feet by 34 feet; the engine and dynamo-room, 54 feet by 62 feet.

The boiler-room contains four boilers, of the Babcock & Wilcox type, of 250 horse-power each, giving a total of 1,000 horse-power. These boilers can be economically worked to 1,250 horse-power.

The furnaces are fitted with the Babcock & Wilcox chain grate, which has a guaranteed efficiency of six and one-half pounds of water evaporated per pound of Illinois slack. It is an automatic stoker, the slack being placed in a hopper and the grate "does the rest." It can be regulated for any depth of fire or velocity of feed desired. The combustion is perfect; no smoke, except when starting a green fire.

In the engine-room are three Buckeye engines, one of 200 and two of 100 horse-power each. These engines are directly coupled to three Siemens & Halske dynamos, one of 140 kilowatts and two of 66 kilowatts each. This electric plant generates the electricity for supplying the light for the Headhouse, train shed, baggage-rooms, express buildings and Station yard, the freight station at Eleventh and Poplar and storage yards, through twenty miles of wire and by 293 arc and 3,500 incandescent lamps.

One engine of 400 horse-power and one dynamo, 500 kilowatts, for lights only, will be added immediately, giving a grand total of 350 arc and 5,000 incandescent lamps, making it probably the largest private electric plant extant.

Two air compressors, of Norwalk & Ingersoll manufacture, of 55 horse-power each, and one small 5 horse-power engine and dynamo are also in the engine-room. These are for compressing air to 80 or 100 pounds pressure and charging a cell storage battery. The compressed air is used for throwing switches and signals, for charging air cylinders on trains in Station, and for pneumatic tube conveyers in Headhouse. The storage battery furnishes electricity for all the interlocking circuits, indicators, buzzers, push-buttons, etc.

One of the Small Fountains.

WAITING ROOM FOR LADIES EXCLUSIVELY.   THOS. C. LINK, Architect.

PART IV.

THE AUXILIARY BUILDINGS.

THE STATION MASTER'S OFFICE.

FRONTING on the Midway, along the iron fence and opposite tracks 15–6, is a kiosk with clock tower. This building contains the office of the station master and a telegraph office, where conductors report for instructions. One panel of its wall on the Midway side has the bulletin board of arriving trains.

BAGGAGE-ROOM BUILDING.

At the Twentieth Street side of the train shed, beginning just south of the Midway, is a two-story building 30 feet wide by 300 feet long. The entire lower floor is used for baggage purposes, excepting 50 feet on the south end, used as a train box-room and employés' closets. The second floor is used for office for general baggage agent; store-room, or "deadhouse," for baggage held over time (reached from the first floor by a large hydraulic elevator); conductors' room, where each road has its bulletins and supplies for conductors; electrical supplies store-room, and railroad mail-rooms.

The walls of the baggage-room, both inside and outside, are lined with boiler-iron to the height of 4 feet all around.

UNITED STATES MAIL ROOM.

Two hundred and thirty feet south of baggage-room building is a two-story, 40x70 feet, building for the handling of United States mail. The transfer clerks, registered letter clerks, distributing clerks and a large force of letter carriers will occupy this building.

This new departure (it being in reality a portion of the St. Louis Post-office) will not only greatly expedite the through mails, but will also save much time in the handling of the city mails.

EXPRESS BUILDINGS.

Lying south of the train shed and east of the track are the express companies' buildings, as follows:

1st—Adams and Southern Express Companies, 150x60 feet.

2d—United States and Pacific Express Companies, 250x60 feet.

3d—American Express Company, 150x60 feet.

4th—Wells-Fargo & Co., 100x60 feet.

Each building has its own track on the Station side, and in the rear a well paved 40-foot street.

THE GENERAL WAITING ROOM ON GROUND FLOOR.

THEO. C. LINK, Architect.

PART V.

INTERLOCKING PLANT.

RAISED on top of the power-house, and occupying the north front, facing the Station track system, is the Interlocking Tower. Here, to a railroad man, is the most interesting spot of any about the terminals. Here is where the combination of brains, air and electricity governs and controls every movement of switch or signal, of engine, train, or car, while on the Union Station tracks within a radius of 1,500 feet from the tower.

The successful operation of the Station depends upon the rapid and safe movement of trains in and out, and the switching of engines, baggage, mail and express cars from one track to another; and when it is stated that, by actual count, 247 distinct movements of trains and engines (requiring 1,600 switches and signals to be thrown) are made in one hour while handling the regular daily traffic, it will be seen that any error of judgment in the selection or planning of the interlocking system would have been a serious one. For this reason great care was necessary in deciding what particular system of interlocking was best for the purpose; bearing in mind the long distances to be covered, the number of switches and signals to be operated, and the consciousness that the operation of the mechanism must be very rapid and absolutely certain in its results, the conclusion was reached that a power plant only would fulfill all of these conditions, and the Westinghouse Electro-Pneumatic System was selected.

The plant consists of: (a) the compressors and electric storage batteries; (b) the interlocking machine; (c) the announcing instruments; (d) the switches and signals.

The compressed air which performs the work of moving the switches and signals is supplied by two compressors of fifty-five horse-power each, furnishing air at eighty pounds pressure per square inch. Only one of these compressors is used at a time, the other being retained for use in cases of emergency. The air is taken from the compressors by a three-inch main

View from Nineteenth Street.

pipe leading to the vicinity of the switches and signals, where it is distributed amongst the individual movements by ¼ inch branch pipes.

The electric storage batteries furnish the current that controls the various switch and signal cylinders, as well as that necessary to operate the announcing instruments in the cabin. There is a nest of thirty cells. The wires from the battery are led to one end of and through the interlocking machine, from whence they are taken to the different switch and signal valves that they control.

The interlocking machine is located in the cabin elevated above the roof of the power-house, so that a view in every direction is possible. It consists of an aggregation of 131 levers dispersed in parallel, longitudinal rows, the upper one containing the switch levers, sixty-six in number, and the lower row consisting of sixty-five signal levers.

On the top of the machine is arranged the interlocking mechanism, which lies in a horizontal plane and consists mainly of the locking shafts, the locking bars and the locks themselves. A locking shaft is connected with each lever and runs from the front to the back of the machine; immediately above the locking shafts are the locking bars, which move back and forth, parallel with the long axis of the machine, and in response to the motion of the particular locking shaft to which each relates. Upon the upper surface of the locking bars are fastened the locking dogs, while carried in brackets at the same height but at right angles to the locking dogs are placed the cross-locks; the latter are not fastened, but are free to move in a direction parallel with the locking shafts and at right angles with the locking bars (see illustration on page 69). The function of the locking is to prevent the movement of any lever until all of the other levers involved with it in any combination shall have first been placed in a certain position. The movement of a lever revolves the locking shaft which drives the locking bar, and through the dogs that are mounted upon it forces certain of the cross-locks into or out of the path of other locking dogs, which ends in holding or releasing the levers with which they are connected. This portion of the work is entirely mechanical. At the end of the locking shaft opposite to that to which the lever is connected is an arrangement which, through an electric lock, prevents the completion of a lever's stroke until the switch or signal shall have first made its entire movement. This acts like a check upon the mechanical locking.

58

VIEW FROM WAITING ROOM FOR LADIES ONLY.   THEO. C. LINK, Architect.

The last important function of the machine is the portion devoted to the making and breaking of the electric circuits which pass between the main battery and the switch and signal valves. This is accomplished by means of vertically placed hard rubber rollers, connected each one of them to one of the locking shafts by beveled gears in such manner that the roller revolves with the motion of the shaft, and in the same direction; upon the periphery of the rollers are placed semicircular phosphor-bronze bands. About two inches back of the rollers, and also in a vertical plane, there is a hard rubber base of a length equal to the length of the machine, and of a width somewhat less than the height of the rollers.

In longitudinal slots on the face of the rubber base long strips of phosphor-bronze are fastened, which at one end of the machine are connected with the battery, and at the other end of the machine are joined with the wires that pass to the various switch and signal valves.

The Interlocking Machine.

Opposite certain rollers the continuity of a strip is interrupted, but the ends of the strips are carried up to a contact with one of the semicircular bands before mentioned; when the roller is in one position both ends of the strip will touch the band, but any movement of the roller from that position will break the contact; therefore, if all of the rollers should be in the correct position, the clearing of a signal or movement of a switch would follow; but if one of the rollers were to be in the wrong position, the signal or switch would not respond, since the signal or switch valve would be cut off from the battery. This, it will be seen, furnishes still another and valuable lock upon the action of the machine as a whole.

Facing the leverman, and extending above the machine, is a model of the tracks, the switches on which are movable, and by a connection with the locking shaft repeat the motion of the switches upon the ground.

In the bay of the cabin are arranged the announcing instruments which inform the director of the condition of the tracks, and instruct him as to what trains are ready to go from and what trains are approaching the depot.

Two fifteen-way semaphore indicators with disc attachments perform a double service; the position of the semaphores indicates whether or not the tracks in the depot are occupied; the discs communicate with push-buttons at the depot and inform the train director when a train is ready to move.

One thirty-way fouling point indicator shows what approaches are blocked by moving trains; two annunciators connected with each leg of the "V" tell the director that certain trains wish to back into the depot, and two other annunciators announce the approach of trains from each direction.

Air whistles controlled from the cabin by electricity are located, one at Eighteenth Street, one at Twenty-first street, and one on signal bridge south of train shed. These whistles are for giving audible signals, stopping engines when "running a signal," expediting movements, calling repairmen, etc.

For purposes not covered by the above, telephone and telegraph instruments are provided.

There are controlled by this plant 119 points, comprising ninety-nine single switches, one single slip, twelve double slips, ten movable frogs, and sixty-eight dwarf signals and thirty-three main line signals. At each of these elements there is located a compressed air cylinder, which through certain mechanism operates the various switches and signals. Connected with each switch cylinder there are three electro-magnets, two of which by means of small pin valves serve to alternately admit and cut off the air to and from either side of the main cylinder valve. The third magnet, which is really nothing but a check upon the other two, is placed between them and just above the cylinder valve; its action is to lock the cylinder valve whenever it is desired that it shall not move.

Briefly, the method of operation is as follows: the switch lever in the machine being in one of its extreme positions, a slight movement of the machine excites the lock magnet and releases the lock at the switch cylinder; a further advance excites one of the outside magnets and discharges the other, which has as a result the shifting of the cylinder valve, the admission of compressed air and the consequent movement of the switch or frog. By continuing the motion of the lever in the cabin, the lock magnet is discharged and the cylinder valve locked in its new position.

The arrangement at the signals is much simpler; since no air pressure is required to restore a signal to the danger position, it is only necessary to interrupt the electric current flowing from the battery to the magnet that is connected with the air cylinder, whereupon the pressure is cut off from the air cylinder and the signal is carried to the danger position by gravity. That is exactly what is done by the movement of the signal lever in the machine from either of its extreme positions to its central or normal position. Connected with each of the switch movements is a device

Interior of Switch Tower.

BASE OF TOWER AND EAST PAVILION.   THEOS. C. LINK, Architect.

62

called a detector bar, whose object is to prevent the movement of any switch or frog while a train stands above it.

In addition to the detector bars, all "fouling points" in the tracks in the Station are electrically indicated, so that when an engine or train is passing over any of these switches or fouling points, or a car or engine is not in far enough to "clear" the other track, the fact is indicated in the tower by a revolving disc (in the thirty-way fouling point indicator) and the levermen can not operate the switches or signals affected by the "fouling."

The signals, both main and dwarf, are lighted by electricity, and four of the main line signals at the throat of the system have blades that are illuminated throughout their entire length and show a position signal by night as well as by day.

Private Dining-Room, Looking East.

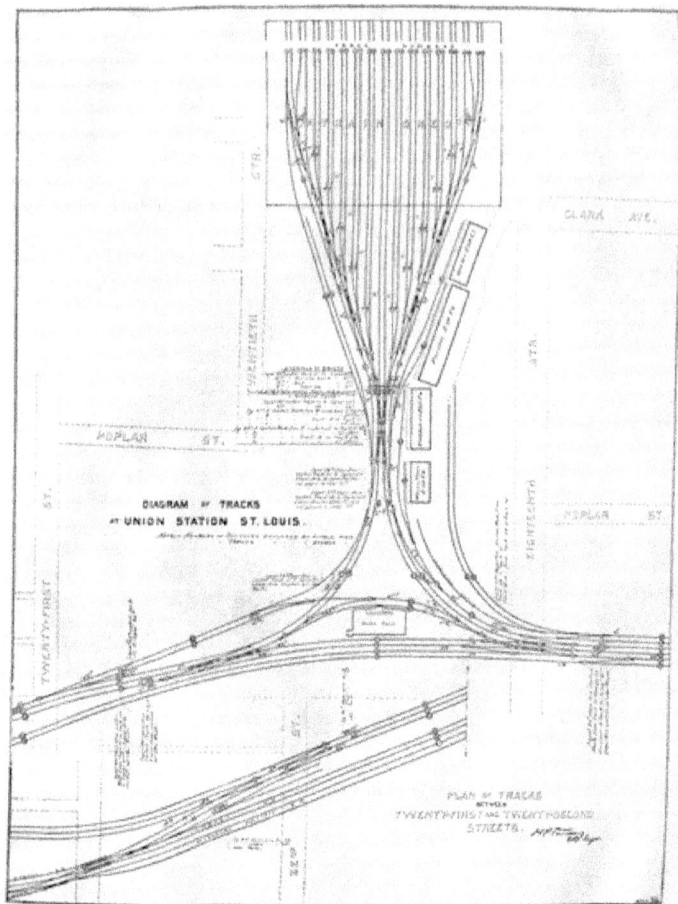

DIAGRAM OF TRACKS
AT UNION STATION ST. LOUIS.

PLAN OF TRACKS
BETWEEN
TWENTY-FIRST AND TWENTY-SECOND
STREETS.

THE MIDWAY.
From Eighteenth Street.

Thos. C. Link, Architect.

PART VI.

OPERATIVE DEPARTMENT.

RECEDING descriptions of the Headhouse, train shed, tracks, etc., have furnished the reader with a fair conception of its architectural, artistic and engineering features. But a railway station must be judged from the standpoint of its utility and the manner of service it gives to the public, and after the architects, artists and engineers have completed their task as to construction of Station, train shed and tracks, it devolves upon the operative department to successfully and satisfactorily operate and administer the plant, and to prove its adaption to the uses and purposes for which it was designed.

The conditions governing the passenger train service at this Station are extremely onerous, owing to the fact that nearly all heavy trains arrive and depart between the hours of 7 to 9 a. m. and 7 to 9 p. m., and the services required at these hours are more difficult to perform than at most Stations.

The St. Louis Union Station, as has already been stated, is of the class known as "End Stations;" i. e., a Station without through tracks, all trains entering and leaving the train shed from one end. There are a number of Stations of this class, but this Station stands alone as being also a "back-in" Station; all trains entering the Station back into it.

While this method of handling trains added largely to the difficulty of planning the track system, and also to the handling of the trains (as trains from the east and west have to be "crossed"), the advantages are as follows:

Main Entrances on Market Street.

(*a*) Engines are kept at the south end of the train shed; smoke and dirt inside of the shed are avoided.

(*b*) Baggage, express and mail cars are concentrated and handled at south end of shed, and there is consequently no trucking on platforms.

(*c*) Increased comfort and safety to passengers, as they are landed direct at the Headhouse free from all danger and annoyance.

These advantages are so great as to fully justify the management in the selection of this method and to amply repay the increased cost, if any, of operating under this system.

It is of interest to note here, that prior to the opening, indeed for a while after, it was confidently predicted by a number of very competent railway officers that the "back-up" plan would never *work*; but the four months' actual operation has convinced even the doubters that it is not only practicable to so operate the Station, but that it is the best system.

By a reference to the plan of the Company's tracks (page 74) it will be seen that its main lines and those of the railroad lines from the west run almost due east and west through Mill Creek Valley, while the Station is located north of and its tracks are at right angles to the said main lines, and are connected with them by double tracks leading east and west.

The thirty tracks in the train shed are accessible from any one of the four main lead tracks, but to secure the greatest possible number of movements of trains at one time these thirty tracks are divided in six primary groups:

First, tracks 1 to 6 inclusive.   Fourth, tracks 16 to 20 inclusive.
Second, tracks 7 to 10 inclusive.   Fifth, tracks 21 to 24 inclusive.
Third, tracks 11 to 15 inclusive.   Sixth, tracks 25 to 30 inclusive.

And these primary groups form four main groups—

First group, 1 and 2, ten tracks for west-bound trains.
Second group, 3, five tracks for trains from the east.
Third group, 4, five tracks for trains from the west.
Fourth group, 5 and 6, ten tracks for east-bound trains.

MARKET STREET PORTE COCHÈRE.

THEOS. C. LINK, Architect.

68

The main lead tracks and cross-overs are so arranged that trains can be moved to or from any one of these four groups at the same moment; thus four trains can be entering and leaving simultaneously, without the slightest interference one with the other.

To fully appreciate the great capacity for handling trains over the comparatively few main lead tracks (four in number) the actual movement of the trains should be seen between the hours of 7 and 9 a. m. from the interlocking tower; the mere statement of the number of movements actually made between these hours (averaging 146 per hour) conveys no adequate idea of the celerity with which the trains are handled.

Prior to the opening of the new Station, the bridge and tunnel tracks were operated in accordance with the general American practice of "Keep to the right," but with the opening of the new Station this had to be changed, as a continuation of this method would have involved the crossing of all trains to and from the east *at the entrance to the Station*, thus not only largely complicating the Station work, but also adding a very serious element of danger; it was, therefore, decided to run "left-handed" to East St. Louis. East-bound passenger trains were, therefore, made to start from the east side (or left-hand side) of the Station, and thus have a *clear* out-bound track, and west-bound trains starting from the west side, and running "right-handed," have also a clear outbound track.

In order that trains may "back in" to Station, trains from the east must run to the west side, and trains from the west to the east side of the Station approaches. East of Eighteenth Street there are three main tracks, Nos. 71, 72 and 73, and west of Twentieth Street are tracks Nos. 70, 71 and 72. Tracks 70 and 71 are *out-bound* tracks for east and west trains. Track 72 to Eighteenth Street, and 71, Eighteenth Street to Twenty-second Street, are for trains *from the east*, and 72 to Eighteenth Street, and 73 from Eighteenth to Fourteenth Street, are for trains *from the west*. A study of the plan of Station tracks will show that a train from the east and one from the west will pass each other running

Porte Cochere on Eighteenth Street.

"right-handed," and only when the train from the west crosses track No. 71 in backing into the Station over track 53 does it cross the track of the train from the east, and then it is moving in the same direction, so that all danger is practically eliminated, even if the interlocking plant should permit of wrong signals.

All train, engine and switching movements are handled direct from the interlocking tower by the director in charge. He has before him on his desk a printed schedule of every regular movement of train, engine, head-end or drag-out, for the twenty-four hours, showing the time it should be

The Telegraph Service.

made, the track from, etc. Before him are his telephone, speaking-tubes, thirty push-buttons for the Station track circuits, and three buttons operating the air whistles at Eighteenth Street, Twenty-second Street and the signal bridge; and to his right and left on each side the "bay" are thirty miniature semaphores, one for each track, with drop discs, which show the condition of the Station tracks, whether occupied or not, and also when the conductor of train "plunges," "ready to start," and thirty larger discs, which show what switches are fouled by standing or passing trains in the Station. Back of him are the levermen, who have such an intimate knowledge of all the possible combinations of the levers that they have all the levers moved almost before the director is through calling the tracks.

ORGANIZATION OF THE SERVICE.

The work of operating and maintaining the property is divided between the departments as follows:

SUPERINTENDENT.—Has charge of all employés and matters connected with the operating of Station, trains and yard work, the superintendent of telegraph, general baggage agent, station master, station director, special agent and general yard master reporting to him on all matters; the master mechanic on matters pertaining to road and yard engine work.

CHIEF ENGINEER.—Has charge of the maintenance and repairs of all tracks, structures, train shed and Headhouse, maintenance of interlocking plant, and also of the electrical department; the superintendent of structure, chief electrician and road master reporting to him.

MASTER MECHANIC.—Has charge of all motive power and power plants, engines, boilers, etc.

PURCHASING AGENT.—Attends to the purchase of all new material and supplies, the sale of old material, and to keeping of records and statistics of this branch. The superintendent, chief engineer, master mechanic, purchasing agent and general ticket agent report direct to the general manager, and he again reports to the President.

SUPERINTENDENT OF TELEGRAPH.—Has charge of all telegraph and telephones, operators and levermen in interlocking towers.

70

SOUTH END OF TRAIN SHED.

THEO. C. LINK, Architect.

71

STATION MASTER.—Has charge of all trains and employés, and the enforcement of all rules inside the train shed. He has direct charge of gatemen, gate police, platform porters and messengers.

STATION DIRECTOR.—Has charge of all the waiting-rooms and public conveniences; the train callers, passenger directors and waiting-room porters and male attendants are under him. He makes a daily morning report to the superintendent of the condition of the building, fixtures and furniture and of any failures of light, heat, any disturbances, etc., during the preceding twenty-four hours.

THE MATRON.—Is in charge of the women's waiting and retiring rooms and attendants. She is also a representative of the Woman's Aid Society, and looks after girls and women who arrive alone and unprotected, and are in need of aid and assistance.

In arranging all the details for the convenience, comfort and information of the traveler, it has been the aim to overlook nothing. In most stations, the greatest difficulty is to find the proper train, and with thirty tracks to hunt over, this is an important item.

To provide for this, all the bulletins show the time of departing trains and also show the numbers of the tracks from which they start. Each track has its sign, which is displayed from fifteen to twenty minutes before leaving time, showing the track number, the train, name of road, destination and leaving time.

The train callers also call the track number, train destination and time.

Arriving trains are bulletined at the station master's office in plain view of everybody, showing whether on time or not; if late, the time they will arrive, and the tracks on which they will come in. Should the track be changed at the last moment, the change is announced at the gate for the track first given.

A *Bureau of Information* is established, facing the Midway in summer and the general waiting-room in winter, in which a special officer is located who answers inquiries from passengers, the range of which is practically unlimited. He is a living bulletin and must be prepared to answer all questions as to trains, routes, facilities, hotels and other matters of general and local concern.

A *Public Telephone* connecting with every firm, corporation, hotel, etc., in the city is at the disposal of the traveling public.

The *Western Union Telegraph Company* occupies a prominent place in the general waiting-room.

A branch *U. S. Post-office* in the main waiting-room furnishes all facilities for mailing or receiving letters, money orders or registered letters at the last moment or while passing through St. Louis.